A Woman's Workshop on JAMES

Books in this series—

A Woman's Workshop on

JAMES

WITH SUGGESTIONS FOR LEADERS

Carolyn Nystrom and Margaret Fromer

ZONDERVAN PUBLISHING HOUSE OF THE ZONDERVAN CORPORATION GRAND RAPIDS, MICHIGAN 49506

A WOMAN'S WORKSHOP ON JAMES
© 1980 by The Zondervan Corporation
Grand Rapids, Michigan

Printed in the United States of America

83   84   85   86   87   88 — 10   9   8   7   6   5

CONTENTS

THE BOOK OF JAMES

James is thought by many to be the first book written for the New Testament, perhaps as early as a dozen years after Christ's death—and written by Christ's own relative. Small wonder that we can almost see the words of Jesus peeking from between the lines.

But while *James* echoes the daily practicality of the Sermon on the Mount, it reaches even further back as the writer instructs a fledgling church. He speaks of "true wisdom" as did King Solomon, and his words, "Come you rich, weep and howl," might well resound from the prophet Amos. James also looks ahead to "the coming of the Lord" as he pleads with his readers to "establish your hearts" in preparation.

Above all, *James* is a book of practice. The writer had no place for a "faith without works." He described such belief quite vividly as "dead." He speaks to daily issues—favoritism, too much money (or too little), sickness, an unruly tongue, interrupted plans, doubt, getting along with other Christians.

The standards are high, so high that once we stretch to reach them, we must at the same time bow in confession of our failure and ask God's help as we stretch again.

James is a demanding book, but a book of wise counsel for anyone who seeks to follow James's Lord. Study it and grow. We did.

—*Maggie and Carolyn*

I'VE JOINED THE GROUP. NOW WHAT?

You've joined a group of people willing to admit that the Bible is worth studying. Some will admit to far more than that —that the Bible is the Word of God and therefore a standard for day-to-day decisions. Others may say that the Bible is merely a collection of interesting teachings and tales, worthy of time and interest but not much more. You may place yourself at one end of this spectrum, or at the other end. Or you may fit somewhere in between. But you have one goal in common with the other people in your group: you believe that the Bible is worth your time, and you hope to enjoy studying it together.

To meet this goal, a few simple guidelines will prevent needless problems.

1. Take a Bible with you. Any modern translation is fine. Suggested versions include: *Revised Standard Version, New*

American Standard Bible, Today's English Version, New International Version, Jerusalem Bible.

A few versions, however, do not work well in group Bible study. For beautiful language, the *King James Version* is unsurpassed. Yours may bear great sentimental value because it belonged to your grandmother. But if you use a *King James,* you will spend a great deal of effort translating the Elizabethan English into today's phrasing, perhaps losing valuable meaning in the process.

Paraphrases like *Living Bible, Phillips,* and *Amplified* are especially helpful in private devotions, but they lack the accuracy of a translation by Bible scholars. Therefore leave these at home on Bible study day.

If you would like to match the phrasing of the questions in this guide, use the *Revised Standard Version.* If, however, you fear that any Bible is far too difficult for you to understand, try *Today's English Version.* This easy-to-read translation is certain to change your mind.

2. Arrive at Bible study on time. You'll feel as if you're half a step behind throughout the entire session if you miss the Bible reading and the opening survey questions.

3. Call your hostess if you are going to be absent. This saves her setting a place for you if refreshments are served. It also frees the group to begin on time without waiting needlessly for you.

4. Volunteer to be a hostess. A quick way to feel as if you belong is to have the Bible study group meet at your house.

5. Decide if you are a talker or a listener. This is a discussion Bible study, and for a discussion to work well all persons should participate more or less equally. If you are a talker, before you speak count ten after the leader asks the question. Try waiting until several other people speak before you give your own point of view.

If you're a listener, remind yourself that just as you benefit from what others say, they profit from your ideas. Besides, your insights will mean more even to you if you put them into words and say them out loud. So take courage and speak.

6. Keep on track. This is a group responsibility. Remember that you are studying the Book of James. Although a speech, magazine article, or some other book may be related, if brought into the conversation it will automatically take time away from the main object of your study, James. In the process, the whole group may go off into an interesting-but-time-consuming tangent, thereby making the leader's job more difficult.

While the Bible is consistent within itself and many excellent topical studies build on its consistency, the purpose of *this* study is to examine thoroughly the Book of James. Therefore cross referencing (comparing sections of James with other portions of Scripture) will cause the same problems as any other tangent. In addition to confusing people who are unfamiliar with other parts of the Bible, cross referencing may cause you to miss James's intent in the passage before you.

For example, James uses the word "justified" in quite a different way than the apostle Paul. To compare passages using this term does a disservice to both authors.

You'll find that each paragraph in James is so laden with facts and ideas that you will be thoroughly challenged to straighten these out without turning to other sections of the Scripture.

Naturally, once you have studied a passage as a group, you

may refer back to it. James assumed his readers had the earlier passage in mind before they read his next section.

7. Help pace the study. With the questions and your Bible in front of you, you can be aware of whether or not the study is progressing at an adequate pace. Each group member shares the responsibility of seeing that the entire passage is covered and the study brought to a profitable close.

8. Don't criticize another church or religion. You might find that the quiet person across the table attends just that church—and she won't be back to your group.

9. Get to know people in your group. Call each other during the week between meetings. Meet socially, share a car pool when convenient, offer to take in a meal if another group member is ill. You may discover that you have more in common than a willingness to study the Bible. Perhaps you'll add to your list of friends.

10. Invite others to the group. Any Bible study group grows best as it absorbs new people and new ideas. So share your new-found interest with a friend or neighbor.

11. Get ready to lead. It doesn't take a mature Bible student to lead this study. Just asking the questions in this guide should prompt a thorough digging into the passage. Besides, you'll find a hefty section of leaders' notes in the back in case you feel a little insecure. So once you've attended the group a few times, sign up to lead a discussion. Remember, the leader learns more than anyone else.

ME, A LEADER?

Sure. Many Bible study groups share the responsibility of leading the discussion. Sooner or later your turn will come. Here are a few pointers to quell any rising panic and help you keep the group working together toward their common goals.

1. Prepare well ahead of time. A week or two in advance is not too much. Read the Scripture passage every day for several successive days. Go over the questions, writing out possible answers in your book. Check the Leaders' Notes on pages 75 to 122 for additional ideas, then read the questions again—several times—until the sequence and wording seem natural to you. Don't let yourself be caught during the study with that now-I-wonder-what-comes-next feeling. Take careful note of the major area of application. Try living it for a week. By then you will discover some of the difficulties others in your group will face when they try to do the same. Finally, pray. Ask God to lead you, as you lead the group. Ask Him to make you sensitive to people, to the Scripture, and to Himself. Expect to grow. You will.

2. Pace the study. Begin on time. People have come for the purpose of studying the Bible. You don't need to apologize for that. At the appointed hour, simply announce that it is time to begin, open with a prayer, and launch into the study.

Keep an eye on the clock throughout the study. These questions are geared to last for an hour to an hour and fifteen minutes. Don't spend forty-five minutes on the first three questions then have to rush through the rest. On the other hand, if the questions are moving by too quickly, the group is probably not discussing each one thoroughly enough. Slow down. Encourage people to interact with each other's ideas. Be sure they are working through all aspects of the question.

Then end—on time. Many people have other obligations immediately after the study and will appreciate a predictable closing time.

3. Ask; don't tell. This study guide is designed for a discussion moderated by a leader. It is *not* a teacher's guide. When you lead the group, your job is like that of a traffic director. You gauge the flow of discussion, being careful that everyone gets a turn. You decide which topics will be treated in what order. You call a halt now and then to send traffic in a new direction. But you do not mount a soapbox and lecture.

Your job is to help each person in the group discover personally the meaning of the passage and to share that discovery with the others. Naturally, since you have prepared the lesson in advance, you will be tempted to tell them all you've learned. Resist this temptation until others have had a chance to discover the same thing. Then, if something is still missing, you may add your own insight to the collection.

4. Avoid tangents. The bane of any discussion group is the oh-so-interesting lure of a tangent. These are always time consuming and rarely as profitable as the planned study. A few red flags will warn you that a tangent is about to arise. They are, "My pastor says . . ."; "I read that . . ."; "The other day Suzie . . ."; "If we look at Ezekiel (or John, or Revelation) . . ."

If this occurs, politely listen to the first few sentences. If these confirm your suspicion that a tangent is indeed brewing, thank the person, then firmly but kindly direct attention back to the passage.

A leader does, however, need to be sensitive to pressing needs within a group. On rare occasions the tangent grows out of a need much more important than any pre-planned study can meet. In these cases, whisper a quick prayer for guidance, and follow the tangent.

5. Talk about application. Each study in this guide leads to a discussion that applies the point of the passage to real life. If you are short of time or if your group feels hesitant in talking about personal things, you'll entertain the thought of omitting these questions. But if you do, your group will lose the main purpose of the study. If God's Word is a book to live by, a few people in your group ought to be willing to talk about how they are going to live in response to it. Putting those intentions into words will strengthen their ability to live out the teachings. The listeners will be challenged to do the same.

So, always allow adequate time to talk over the application questions. Be prepared also to share your own experiences as you have tried to live out the passage.

6. Try a prayer 'n' share. Many groups start their session with fifteen minutes of coffee, then hold a short time of sharing personal concerns, needs, and answers to prayer. Afterward, the group members pray briefly for each other, giving thanks and praise, and asking together that God will meet the needs expressed. These short informal sentence prayers are much like casual sharing conversation. The group members simply turn their conversation away from each other and toward God. For many, this brief time of prayer becomes a weekly life line.

7. Enjoy leading. It's a big responsibility, but one that is rewarding.

1

WILL TRIAL TAKE AWAY MY FAITH?

James 1:1–12

1. If you were beginning to doubt God during a time of trial, what questions might you be asking about Him?

_____

_____

_____

Read aloud James 1:1–8.

2. From James's instructions, what kind of problems do you think he had in mind? (Indicate what phrases in the passage make you think this.) _____

_____

_____

_____

_____

If you were having a hard time maintaining your faith because of trying circumstances, what would be your first response if a friend wrote you the words of verse 2? _____

_____

3. In verses 2–4, what difference do you see between James's attitude toward trial and yours? _____

_____

_____

_____

4. How do you think trials might change you so you would become a more mature person? _____

_____

_____

_____

Read again verses 5–8.

5. What picture does James use to illustrate a doubter?

_____

_____

How would this person behave? _____

_____

_____

_____

6. What reasons might a person have to hesitate about coming to God for wisdom? _____

_____

_____

Where might he look for help instead? _____

_____

_____

7. Recall your answer to question 1, your doubts about God when you are in a time of trial. Why would it be harder for the doubter of verses 5–8 to receive God's wisdom than the person described in verses 2–4? _____

_____

_____

_____

Read aloud verses 9–12.

8. How might getting rich or becoming poor test your faith? _____

_____

_____

_____

9. What besides money is important enough to you to be a test of your faith? _____

_____

_____

_____

10. How does the word *endure* in verse 12 change your view of what to expect of God during a period of trial?

_____

_____

_____

11. How might the first twelve verses of James help you in rearranging your priorities? _____

_____

_____

_____

12. Bring to mind the biggest trial you are now facing. How is it a test of your faith? _____

_____

_____

_____

_____

13. Taking the teaching of this passage into account, spend five minutes writing out a prayer for God's help in your present circumstances. (When everyone has finished, there will be time for you together to pray your prayers silently to the Lord.) _____

_____

_____

_____

_____

_____

_____

_____

_____

_____

_____

Read James 1:4 aloud, then sing together the following song of encouragement.

Complete In Thee

CECIL F. ALEXANDER

HEINRICH C. ZEUNER

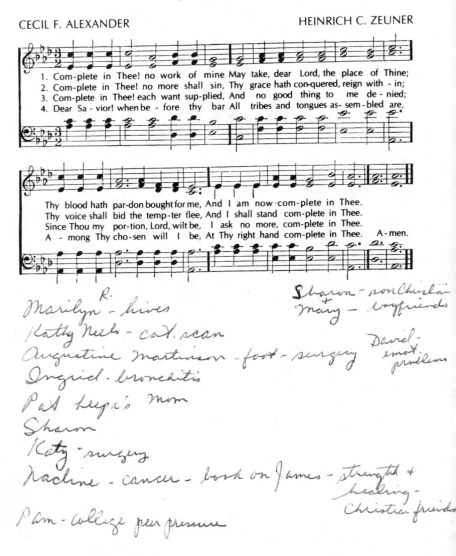

1. Com-plete in Thee! no work of mine May take, dear Lord, the place of Thine;
2. Com-plete in Thee! no more shall sin, Thy grace hath con-quered, reign with - in;
3. Com-plete in Thee! each want sup-plied, And no good thing to me de - nied;
4. Dear Sa - vior! when be - fore thy bar All tribes and tongues as-sem-bled are,

Thy blood hath par-don bought for me, And I am now·com-plete in Thee.
Thy voice shall bid the temp-ter flee, And I shall stand com-plete in Thee.
Since Thou my por-tion, Lord, wilt be, I ask no more, com-plete in Thee.
A - mong Thy cho-sen will I be, At Thy right hand com-plete in Thee. A-men.

2

HOW CAN I FIND JOY IN TRIAL?

James 1:12–18

1. What are some of the things that make your life worth-while? _____ *Jesus & having fellowship w/ Him, Bible, food good, nice home, mother, friends, church, a vision*

Read James 1:12–18.

2. People sometimes say that a person is "tried and true." What does this mean? *V. 12 - persevered under trial - like Job, will not curse god under most trying circumstances*

How might this expression help you understand verse 12?

_____

_____

22

3. What to you is the major difference in the trials God sends (vv. 1–4, 12) and the temptations described in verses 13–15? *Temptations are when our sin nature is enticed to do evil – self is foremost; trials god sends are when man overcomes sin nature, + perseverance wins out*

4. Why are words like *tempt, lure,* and *entice* appropriate descriptions of the way desire and sin seek to capture us?

Satan can appear as an angel of light + make sin look v. attractive

5. How do you see the downward slide described in verses 13–15 working out in a practical way? *girls dating guys they shouldn't*

6. Think of some of your answers to question 1, the things that seemed to make your life worthwhile. How might these desires lure you away from God? *food – lack of self-control in 1 area leads to lack of it in others; home – valuing material possessions more than my spiritual possession – Jesus – which no one can take away*

only every good & perfect gift is fm. God

7. We see good things in the lives of many people. How might we be deceived about their source? _Success, money look good in the eyes of the world but are they god's best plan for one - sometimes not - Satan will give success if it distracts fm. god_

8. What in your experience has made you feel out of touch with the gifts God, in His kindness, gives us? _When I look only at what I can see, I can forget the many unseen things He's given me - when doubt & disbelief creep in_

9. When we feel out of touch, we sometimes say, "God doesn't seem to care about me any more." What answers to this does James pose in verses 16–18? _As surely as god made the sun & the moon & stars & as surely as they appear every day, so He is the same - not like shifting shadows, always there_

sun = god's dependability

clouds

10. When a person is in a period of depression, what changes in attitude might be experienced as a result of responding to the God of these verses? _confess lack of perseverance, evil desires then thank Him for what He's given us seen & unseen, esp. Jesus → joy, gratefulness will result -emotions will follow - Joni thanked Him in obed. to the Word -emotions followed_

11. Suppose we know in our minds that this passage is true, but we don't feel it in our emotions. What actions can we take to bring our feelings in line with the truth? (Consider what you can say to God, what you might sing, ways to keep up with routine activities, things you can do that are likely to encourage joy.) *Obey & He'll bring about the emotions; play records, listen to WRBS*

3

IS MY RELIGION TRUE?

James 1:18–27

Read James 1:18–27.

As you read, particularly notice James's references to God's Word.

1. What can you find out about the *Word* from these references? Mention as many things as possible. _____

_____

_____

_____

_____

Of what value might this kind of Word be to you? _____

_____

_____

_____

Read silently verses 19–21.

2. Imagine a person who does just the opposite of the three commands in verse 19. What problems does he create for those around him? _____

_____

_____

_____

_____

For himself? _____

_____

Why might his relation with God be difficult? _____

_____

_____

3. Why might a person, honestly seeking to do God's work, need these instructions? _____

_____

_____

_____

How might he benefit from them? _____

_____

_____

4. In what ways is the person of verse 21 a contrast to the one you described from verse 19? _____

_____

_____

How can this attitude of submission or meekness be a dynamic force rather than a passive one? _____

_____

_____

_____

Look again at verses 22–25.

5. In what ways might a person who has learned the lesson of verses 19–21 still be deceiving himself? _____

_____

_____

6. Why do you think a mirror is a good illustration of God's Word? _____

_____

_____

_____

7. According to these verses, what ought to be the results when we see ourselves mirrored in God's Word? _____

_____

_____

_____

_____

8. What patterns can we develop in our use of Scripture that will help us to look at God's Word and be changed?

_____

_____

_____

Read verses 26–27.

9. How can you deceive yourself by talking too much?

_____

_____

_____

_____

10. According to these verses, what are the differences between vain and true religion? _____

_____

_____

_____

_____

11. How might the person described in verse 19 be well qualified to help needy people? _____

_____

_____

_____

12. How is a worldly spirit in conflict with the attitude described here? (Use the entire passage.) _____

_____

_____

_____

13. Bring to mind one relationship that might be healed by this Scripture passage (a relationship with a person, a group of people, God). What specific change can you initiate in response to its teachings?

_____

_____

_____

_____

_____

on eating a cake all by yourself*

as soon as she said
". . . so lonely. . . ."
I talked warmly
as fast as I could
about gardening and church
fellowship
and convenient shopping centers
and Red Cross volunteer work
and good TV programs and
the Friend Closer Than a Brother
and others more needy
than she.
then, depositing the flowered
cake tin
on the kitchen counter
(neat as the numeral "1") I
left

—*Luci Shaw*

_____

*Reprinted from *Listen to the Green*, © Luci Shaw 1971, Harold Shaw Publishers, Wheaton, Illinois 60187. Used by permission.

4

HOW DO I MEASURE A PERSON'S WORTH?

James 2:1–13

Read aloud James 2:1–7.

1. If you were a visitor in this church, what would you hear and see? _____

_____

_____

_____

_____

2. Why do you think the people behaved this way?

_____

_____

_____

_____

3. What two inconsistencies in their behavior does James point out in verses 5–7? _____

_____

_____

_____

4. If all these people became part of the same congregation, what problems can you see arising? _____

_____

_____

_____

5. In what ways has each person involved (rich, poor, church member, the Lord Himself) been dishonored?

_____

_____

_____

_____

6. How does the title James gives Jesus in verse 1 help set this behavior in perspective? _____

_____

_____

_____

7. What reasons do you give yourself for showing more favor to some people than to others? _____

_____

_____

_____

_____

How are your values in this area different from God's?

_____

_____

_____

Read aloud James 2:8–13.

8. How does verse 8 define the royal law? _____

_____

_____

9. How do these verses answer you when you argue that showing partiality is only a small fault? _____

_____

_____

_____

10. What responsibilities does being under a law of *liberty* place on a person? _____

_____

_____

_____

_____

11. How does your own need for a judgment of mercy help you avoid the temptation to show partiality? _____

_____

_____

_____

_____

_____

12. The royal law can help us resist temptation to show partiality. In what ways do you love and care for yourself?

_____

_____

_____

_____

_____

Think of one person you tend to ignore. (This could be a family member, neighbor, church friend, or working associate.) _____

_____

What might you do to show love to this person? _____

_____

_____

_____

_____

_____

_____

How Do I Love Me?*

How do I love me? Let me count the ways:

I see "me" as a good person. I know that I don't always do the right thing. I know that there are many times when I hurt other people with my words and actions. But I know that hurting people is not what I want to do. So, when I've caused someone pain, I feel badly; but I always forgive me. Then I go back to seeing me as a basically good person. If I didn't, how could I possibly live with myself?

Because I love myself, I want to be a better person. I take pride in the things I can do well. And, I want to improve myself so I'll do even better. I take the time necessary to discipline myself so I will become better in the ways I want to become better.

Because I love me, I think I am right about most everything. When someone tells me I'm wrong, I take a look at myself. "Myself," I say, "are you or are you not right?" If I've been wrong, I admit to me (and to others). Then I try to be right again by changing my ways. When I am convinced that I am not wrong, I stick up for me.

I clothe my body. I keep it warm. I want other people to think I look nice, so I try to dress pleasingly.

Because I love me, I don't gossip about me. I try to show others my best side. I put me in the best light in front of others. And when I do tell others about my bad qualities, or about some "goof" I've made, I only tell those who I am certain will understand, forgive and continue to accept me. With other people I "dummy up." I only tell them the good things about me because I know they will use the bad things to hurt me.

Because I love me, I provide for my body's needs. I feed me when I am hungry. My body needs nourishment if it is to remain alive and well. I give it what it needs.

Because I love me, I seek to expose myself to pleasant things.

Because I love me, I avoid feelings that are disagreeable. I hate burnt toast and sour milk.

Because I love me, I often wonder why other people hurt me so easily. I wonder how they can pass me by without showing compassion—without helping me. I wonder how they can ignore me when I am reaching out to them.

Yes, I love me very much! I'll admit it. It is true! Should I deny it? And what is so bad about that? I show my love for me every moment, in every action. And while I am counting the ways in which I love me, I am overwhelmed by Jesus' command, "Love your neighbor in the same way you love yourself."

—*Raymond Foster*

*Reprinted by permission of *Eternity* magazine, © 1979, Evangelical Ministries, Inc., 1716 Spruce Street, Philadelphia, Pa. 19103.

5

IS MY FAITH DEAD OR ALIVE?

James 2:14–26

1. If you were asked the question, "What use is your faith?" what could you say? _____

_____

_____

_____

Read aloud James 2:14–17.

2. Today's study speaks of two kinds of faith. What are the characteristics of the faith described in verses 14–17?

_____

_____

_____

_____

3. To what extent has this person responded to God?

_____

_____

Read aloud James 2:18–26.

4. A person might offer a list of biblical beliefs to prove he was really a Christian. List some truths that a Christian believes. _____

_____

_____

_____

_____

Which of these beliefs might the demons share? _____

_____

_____

5. From verses 18–20, what can you know about any belief that does not affect behavior? _____

_____

_____

_____

6. What illustrations does James bring from the Old Testament to support his argument? _____

_____

_____

_____

Read again verses 18–24.

7. How would you answer the argument raised in verse 18 that Abraham was justified either by faith alone or by works alone? _____

_____

_____

_____

_____

Additional information about Abraham: God promised that his son, Isaac, would become a great nation. Later, God commanded Abraham to offer his son as a burnt offering. Abraham willingly obeyed God's command. God intervened at the last moment and substituted a ram for the offering.

8. What would have to come about for you to say of someone, "He is a friend of God"? _____

_____

_____

_____

_____

9. If you were to try this week to be a better friend of God, what would you do or not do? _____

_____

_____

_____

_____

_____

10. What did Rahab believe about God? (See Joshua 2:1–15.) _____

_____

_____

_____

How did she show it? _____

_____

_____

_____

11. What qualities in faith did Abraham, the father of his nation, have in common with Rahab, the prostitute?

_____

_____

_____

12. James 2:18–24 speaks of two kinds of faith: dead faith and living faith. From the information in these verses, how would you define each? _____

_____

_____

_____

13. In what ways is saving faith saying, "I believe"?

_____

_____

_____

In what ways is it more than saying, "I believe"? _____

_____

_____

_____

14. What is your one pressing job this week? _____

_____

How might you better express your faith as you do that work?

_____

_____

_____

_____

_____

May the Mind of Christ My Saviour

KATIE B. WILKINSON   A. CYRIL BARHAM-GOULD

1. May the mind of Christ my Sav-iour Live in me from day to day,
   By His love and pow'r con-trol-ling All I do and say.
2. May the Word of God dwell rich-ly In my heart from hour to hour,
   So that all may see I tri-umph On-ly thro' His pow'r.
3. May the peace of God my Fa-ther Rule my life in e-v'ry thing,
   That I may be calm to com-fort Sick and sor-row-ing.
4. May the love of Je-sus fill me, As the wa-ters fill the sea;
   Him ex-alt-ing, self a-bas-ing, This is vic-to-ry.
5. May I run the race be-fore me, Strong and brave to face the foe,
   Look-ing on-ly un-to Je-sus As I on-ward go.
6. May His beau-ty rest up-on me As I seek the lost to win,
   And may they for-get the chan-nel, See-ing on-ly Him. A-men.

Words and music by permission of C. Barham-Gould.

6

DO I HAVE TONGUE TROUBLE?

James 3:1–12

1. If you could replay the conversation around your dinner table last night, what would your talk reveal about you?

_____

_____

_____

Read aloud James 3:1–12.

2. What responsibilities does God give a spiritual teacher? (Consider knowledge, skills, relationships, etc.) _____

_____

_____

_____

_____

3. Why would God impose strict standards and strict judgment on teachers? _____

_____

_____

_____

_____

4. Why is disciplined speech a mark of spiritual maturity?

_____

_____

_____

5. Find three illustrations James uses to describe the tongue in verses 3–5. _____

_____

_____

_____

What qualities of the tongue is he emphasizing? _____

_____

_____

_____

6. Mention a time when what someone said gave your life direction. _____

_____

_____

_____

_____

7. When has what you said controlled you? _____

_____

_____

_____

8. What pictures does James use in verses 6–10 to show the negative nature of speech? _____

_____

_____

_____

What qualities of the tongue are suggested by these verses?

_____

_____

_____

Note: Cycle of nature (v. 6) refers to the whole course of life from birth to death.

9. Think of one conflict situation you have experienced. (In the neighborhood—garden-lovers versus kid-lovers; in business—a landlord not keeping up with repairs as agreed; at home—a child's persistent uncooperativeness with assigned jobs.) How did what you said in that situation illustrate one of these destructive qualities of speech cited by James?

_____

_____

_____

_____

_____

Read aloud verses 9–12.

10. What are some reasons given here why God might not accept your praise? _____

_____

_____

11. Evaluate your speech habits. (Consider particularly the way you talk to your family, casual conversation, comments in Bible study.) In view of this passage, what would you like to change? _____

_____

_____

_____

_____

12. What can you do to make your speech valuable—both useful to others and acceptable to God? _____

_____

_____

_____

_____

O For a Thousand Tongues

CHARLES WESLEY   CARL G. GLASER (LOWELL MASON, ARR.)

1. O for a thou-sand tongues to sing My great Re-deem-er's praise, The glo - ries of my God and King, The tri - umphs of His grace.
2. My gra - cious Mas - ter and my God, As-sist me to pro-claim, To spread through all the earth a-broad, The hon - ors of Thy name.
3. Je - sus! the name that charms our fears, That bids our sor-rows cease; 'Tis mu - sic in the sin-ner's ears, 'Tis life, and health, and peace.
4. He breaks the power of can - celed sin, He sets the pris - oner free; His blood can make the foul-est clean; His blood a-vailed for me.
5. Hear Him, ye deaf; His praise, ye dumb, Your loos-ened tongues em-ploy; Ye blind, be-hold your Sav-iour come; And leap, ye lame, for joy. A-men.

7

HOW CAN I LIVE OUT GOD'S WISDOM?

James 3:13–18

1. Who do you think of as a wise person? _____

_____

What makes you think this person is wise? _____

_____

_____

_____

Read aloud James 3:13–18.

2. According to verse 13, what will mark a wise person?

_____

Why might real wisdom have these results? _____

_____

_____

3. What are the source and characteristics of each of the two kinds of wisdom studied in this passage? _____

_____

_____

_____

_____

4. In what ways can Christians be jealous of each other?

_____

_____

_____

_____

_____

5. How can jealousy and ambition cause disorder in a church? _____

_____

_____

_____

_____

_____

How might a good ambition lead to selfish expression?

_____

_____

_____

_____

_____

6. Growing Christians should have spiritual ambitions. What are some of your spiritual ambitions? _____

_____

_____

_____

_____

What do you need to be careful about in order to keep these ambitions from creating disorder? _____

_____

_____

_____

7. Why do you think the word "pure" is the first characteristic of wisdom from above? _____

_____

_____

_____

_____

8. Contrast again the two kinds of wisdom. Find differences in the way a person relates to other Christians.

_____

_____

_____

In the way he relates to God. _____

_____

_____

In the consequences of his wisdom. _____

_____

_____

9. Look again at the list of words describing God's wisdom. Select one and tell why this way of dealing with people is both wise and practical. _____

_____

_____

_____

_____

_____

10. Think of one situation where you have the option of bringing either peace or disorder. If you are to exercise godly wisdom, what course of action will you take? _____

_____

_____

_____

_____

_____

8

HOW DO I GET WHAT I NEED?

James 4:1–10

1. What methods do people use to get what they want?

_____

_____

Read aloud James 4:1–10.

2. What causes fighting among Christians? (Find eight to ten answers in the passage.) _____

_____

_____

_____

_____

_____

_____

3. What words in verses 1 and 2 show the intensity of this conflict? _____

_____

_____

How might one believer "murder" another? _____

_____

_____

4. How are the people of verses 1–4 exhibiting a desire to be friends with the world? _____

_____

_____

_____

Why do you think *unfaithful creatures* (v. 4) is an appropriate description? _____

_____

_____

5. What good spiritual goals can you think of which God might not honor if our motives were selfish? _____

_____

_____

_____

6. According to verses 1–6, how might a person go about becoming an enemy of God? _____

_____

_____

_____

What would this person gain and what would he lose?

_____

_____

_____

Read again verses 6–10.

7. Contrast in as many ways as you can the person described in verses 1–3 with the person in verses 7–10.

_____

_____

_____

_____

8. Why might some people choose to be double-minded?

_____

_____

_____

What problems does this pose? (See also James 1:8.)

_____

_____

_____

9. James says the alternative to meeting our needs through friendship with the world is submission to God (James 4:7). Which actions in verses 7–10 describe this submission?

_____

_____

_____

10. In what ways is resisting Satan different than running from him? _____

_____

_____

_____

11. According to verses 8–10, what can you expect to happen when you draw near to God? (What will you do? What will He do?) _____

_____

_____

_____

_____

12. Have a time of silent prayer. (See instructions for conducting this in Leaders' Notes, pages 105–107.)

† † †

LORD of all power and might, who art the author and giver of all good things; Graft in our hearts the love of thy Name, increase in us true religion, nourish us with all goodness, and of thy great mercy keep us in the same; through Jesus Christ our Lord. Amen.

—*The Book of Common Prayer,* 1781

9

ARE MY PLANS GOD'S PLANS?

James 4:11–17

Read aloud James 4:11–17.

   1. What examples of arrogance do you find here?

_____

_____

_____

_____

   2. How has the person of verses 11 and 12 overstepped his position? _____

_____

_____

_____

_____

3. What do James's previous teachings contribute to your understanding of God's view of speaking evil against someone? (See especially James 2:8–10 and 3:9–11.) _____

_____

_____

_____

_____

4. What might speaking evil against someone include?

_____

_____

_____

_____

5. What mistakes have the people in verses 13–17 made?

_____

_____

_____

_____

6. What is a "lord"? _____

_____

What would the relationship be like between you and someone who was your lord? _____

_____

_____

_____

_____

7. How is your life like a mist? _____

_____

Why did these people need to be reminded that life is a mist?

_____

_____

_____

_____

8. In what way does having Jesus as your Lord bring substance to life? _____

_____

_____

_____

_____

9. When has something you planned and desired, failed to materialize? _____

_____

_____

_____

_____

_____

How do you react when your plans don't work out? _____

_____

_____

_____

_____

10. Note briefly in writing:

My plan for tomorrow _____

_____

_____

My plan for ten years from now _____

_____

_____

11. How should an earnest belief that Jesus is your Lord affect these plans and your attitude toward them? _____

_____

_____

_____

_____

Have Thine Own Way, Lord

ADELAIDE A. POLLARD

GEO. C. STEBBINS

1. Have thine own way, Lord! Have thine own way! Thou art the Pot-ter; I am the clay. Mold me and make me aft-er thy will While I am wait-ing, yield-ed and still.
2. Have thine own way, Lord! Have thine own way! Search me and try me, Mas-ter, to-day! Whit-er than snow, Lord, wash me just now, As in thy pres-ence hum-bly I bow.
3. Have thine own way, Lord! Have thine own way! Wound-ed and wea-ry, help me, I pray! Pow-er—all pow-er—sure-ly is thine! Touch me and heal me, Sav-iour di-vine!
4. Have thine own way, Lord! Have thine own way! Hold o'er my be-ing ab-so-lute sway! Fill with thy Spir-it till all shall see Christ on-ly, al-ways, liv-ing in me!

10

DO MY POSSESSIONS CRY OUT AGAINST ME?

James 5:1–12

Read aloud James 5:1–6.

1. What are the miseries for which the rich will weep and howl? _____

_____

_____

_____

_____

2. What crimes does the evidence point to? _____

_____

_____

_____

_____

3. According to these verses, what is wrong with the way these people viewed possessions? _____

_____

_____

_____

Read aloud James 5:7–12.

4. How might believers view Christ's return differently than the corrupt rich? _____

_____

_____

_____

5. What is ironic about laying up treasure for the last days as verse 3 accuses the rich of doing? _____

_____

_____

_____

6. Find three examples of patience in this passage.

_____

_____

_____

What reason does each suggest for not wanting to hasten the return of the Lord? _____

_____

_____

_____

7. What are some instructions that James gives to oppressed believers? _____

_____

_____

_____

_____

_____

8. How might these instructions aid believers in their relationships with each other? _____

_____

_____

_____

_____

What effect would obeying these instructions have on their relationship with God? _____

_____

_____

_____

_____

9. How is God's judgment evidence of his compassion and mercy? _____

_____

_____

_____

_____

10. What do you look forward to in Christ's return?

_____

_____

_____

What do you fear about it? _____

_____

_____

_____

11. In a democratic society, each person has some responsibility for the oppressed. What cries from your own community might now be reaching the ears of the Lord of Hosts?

_____

_____

_____

_____

12. What measures can you take to keep these cries from being evidence before God against you? _____

_____

_____

_____

_____

_____

Prophet*

His voice is heat-wave thunder
unannounced, a long way off,
a break in the skyscape,
a dreary day respite,
a hint that things may change.

He scares me at times,
the deepness, low, growlly,
fanged prelude to rainstorm
and uncertain crops.

I wish he'd not come.
We have priest and king;
they don't rumble so
and wake me at night.
God knows I need my rest.

—*Carolyn Keefe*

*Reprinted by permission of *Eternity* magazine, © 1978, Evangelical Ministries, Inc., 1716 Spruce Street, Philadelphia, Pa. 19103.

11

WHY DO I NEED OTHER CHRISTIANS?

James 5:13–20

Read aloud James 5:13–20.

1. How should a Christian respond differently to life's circumstances than a non-believer? _____

_____

_____

_____

_____

2. In the drama of verses 14–15, what part does each person play? _____

_____

_____

_____

3. What qualities would an elder need in order to perform this function? _____

_____

_____

_____

4. Why do you think the Lord honors this procedure?

_____

_____

_____

_____

5. Using the whole passage, in what ways are Christians to be responsible for one another? _____

_____

_____

_____

_____

6. What value might there be in confession of sin to a fellow believer? _____

_____

_____

_____

What is the difference between sharing and confession?

_____

_____

_____

7. Why is righteousness a condition for power in prayer?

_____

_____

_____

8. What encouragement does the example of Elijah give?

_____

_____

_____

_____

9. If you were to wander from the truth, what kind of help might bring you back? _____

_____

_____

_____

_____

10. Glance again through the entire passage. What do you need from the kind of Christian support described here?

_____

_____

_____

_____

What could you bring to such a support system? _____

_____

_____

_____

11. In what ways is your church fulfilling these functions?

_____

_____

_____

If your church were to better follow these patterns for supporting each other in Christian growth, what changes would need to take place? _____

_____

_____

_____

_____

Blest Be the Tie

JOHN FAWCETT   HANS G. NAEGELI

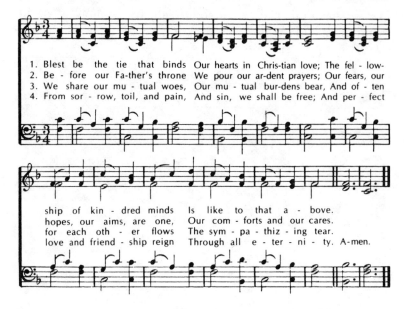

1. Blest be the tie that binds Our hearts in Chris-tian love; The fel - low-
2. Be - fore our Fa-ther's throne We pour our ar-dent prayers; Our fears, our
3. We share our mu - tual woes, Our mu - tual bur-dens bear, And of - ten
4. From sor - row, toil, and pain, And sin, we shall be free; And per - fect

ship of kin - dred minds Is like to that a - bove.
hopes, our aims, are one, Our com - forts and our cares.
for each oth - er flows The sym - pa - thiz - ing tear.
love and friend - ship reign Through all e - ter - ni - ty. A-men.

12

HOW CAN I KNOW IF I'M A CHRISTIAN?

Ephesians 2:1–10

1. What encouragement have you found for walking right-eously as you have studied James? _____

_____

_____

_____

_____

In what ways has James's standard for living seemed dis-couraging? _____

_____

_____

_____

_____

Read Ephesians 2:1–10.

2. Describe the problem Paul presents in the first three verses. (Include origin, scope, and characteristics.) _____

_____

_____

_____

_____

3. What modern attitudes and interests illustrate what Paul had in mind? _____

_____

_____

_____

_____

4. In describing anyone so obviously lively, why would Paul use the word "dead"? _____

_____

_____

_____

5. What characteristics of God are mentioned in verses 4–10, and how is each particularly important in view of the situation? _____

_____

_____

_____

_____

_____

6. What actions did God take to solve the problem?

_____

_____

7. What does Paul mean here when he says a person has been "saved"? _____

_____

_____

_____

_____

_____

8. Who is the active person in the first three verses in contrast to the active person in the last verses? _____

_____

_____

_____

What reason for this change is implied in the passage?

_____

_____

_____

9. What is the difference between the "works" mentioned in verse 9 and those mentioned in verse 10? _____

_____

_____

_____

_____

10. What would you expect the loyalties of a Christian to be, in contrast to those of the "dead" described in verses 1–3? _____

_____

_____

_____

11. How might a confidence in your own goodness keep you from being saved? _____

_____

_____

12. What are some things you are alive to now, that you were not alive to before you became a Christian? _____

_____

_____

_____

13. Suppose a person said to you, "What do I have to do to be saved?" How would you answer that person from the information in this passage? _____

_____

_____

_____

_____

NOTES TO LEADERS

1

Will Trial Take Away My Faith?

James 1:1–12

Hard times in our circumstances result in spiritual hard times as well. We ask ourselves: If God really cares, where is He? Why is this happening? What difference does being a Christian make? James does not directly answer *these* questions, but he does tell us a lot about how to meet trials with a courage and hope that results in spiritual growth. We do not need to be diminished by the pressures of life.

Pray for the people in your study group. Pray that those who are under pressure will be given courage to meet life with joyful endurance and faith in God. Ask that He will give them the desire to be steadfast and that their steadfastness will have its full effect—their perfect completeness in Jesus Christ.

1. It is hard to admit doubts about God even to ourselves. To get reactions that are as true to life as possible, this ques-

tion should be discussed before the passage is read. It will introduce the whole area of discussion—the spiritual dimension of hardship. The question is phrased to assume that all of us, even "good Christians," have doubts about God. The passage assumes that it is all right to admit these doubts and learn how to deal with them. If this question is handled realistically, the answers the passage gives will be useful to each person, not just something for a "weaker brother" or something applying to a future event.

2. This question particularly refers to the instructions found in verses 2–4. The problems sound like ones people run into or "meet" in the course of daily living rather than inner temptations to sin. And the problems seem to be of all different sorts and, therefore, quite unpredictable. They could have been trials of sickness or finances or loneliness. Christians also undoubtedly faced the pressure of trying to live uprightly in a world that wanted everyone to try to get away with as much as possible.

Someone in your Bible study may mention that James was writing to Jews of the Dispersion (verse 1) and may have had particular problems in mind because of this. The term "dispersion" is used to refer to Jews scattered throughout the non-Jewish world. A voluntary scattering began as early as the time of Solomon, but it was intensified when Israel was overrun by the conquering kings of Babylon and Assyria. By the time of the New Testament there were communities of faithful Jews throughout the known world.

The Book of Acts shows Paul regularly opening his evangelistic work in Gentile nations by preaching in the synagogue. Here, James is not speaking to the Jews as a race, but to Christian Jews who are undergoing trials and testings because they have accepted the Lord Jesus Christ as Messiah.

They received not only the pagan world's distrust of both Christians and Jews, but the scorn of their unconverted Jewish neighbors as well.

Quick spontaneous reactions are what you need for the second part of question 2; just enough to form a basis for the next question. Guard against spending too much time on a long chronicle of past hurts.

3. James feels that trials are a positive experience to be met with joy and expectancy. He implies that without some trials we remain immature. If your group is not exploring the possibilities of these verses sufficiently, you might ask, "Why does James think trials can be looked at joyfully?"

4. The answers to this question will be personal. However, several areas of discussion might reflect that trials often give us greater sensitivity to other people, an ability to understand and be of practical help to them. Trials cause us to talk to and depend more on the Lord; they can help us appreciate and find comfort in His presence. They are likely to build courage, strength, and resourcefulness. Perhaps some members of your group have practical examples of the way hardship has actually taught them a useful lesson. These would be helpful to the group. Encourage brevity, however.

5. The illustration of a wave driven by the wind is like a person who can't make up his mind. He is filled with uncertainty and indecision. He probably believes in God but cannot decide whether he should follow God's way or do something more "practical." He may be irritable because of this unsettledness. Or he may make promises which he then unmakes when he changes his mind. Your group should be able to think of a number of specific examples.

6. Perhaps a person would hesitate to ask God for wisdom because he isn't sure whether God will give him what he needs. He might have refused to go God's way often enough so that he feels as though he no longer has a right to ask. (The words "generously" and "without reproach" lend themselves to these ideas.) Maybe he is afraid that he won't like God's way of doing things.

Some typical places we look for advice are from friends and neighbors, our own instinctive feelings, a school of worldly philosophy. This does not exclude other avenues of advice and knowledge, but the believer's attitude should be that all real sense of direction comes from God and He is the ultimate source of truth. It is an attitude of supplication, dependency, and humility.

7. Often verse 6 is quoted out of context, as though we could have any request answered if we could drum up enough faith. Verse 6 should be read with verse 5. When life presses on us with decisions that have to be made, we can ask wisdom from God. But we must ask without a double mind, wanting partly our own way and partly God's way; or wanting to know what God would say but reserving for ourselves the right to decide whether to follow his way or not. Doubt about God and His goodness seems to produce a climate in which prayers for wisdom cannot be answered. We need to come to Him believing He will deal with our problem, come expecting some benefit from God. This teaching in James is not unlike Jesus' comment after a miraculous healing, "Thy faith has made thee well."

8, 9. Even though wealth is short-lived and transitory, it is hard not to over-value it and trust it for our security and happiness. We are also likely to trust our security in things other than riches. These could include our husband and children, social position, a good job, education, or health. A Christian has glimpsed life's true values and should be in a better position to accept from the hand of a trustworthy God whatever life offers.

10. Often we pray for release from our problems and are disappointed when God does not change our circumstances. This need for endurance might lead us to ask instead for wisdom to handle the situation, for patience, and for strength. The person who does endure through trial is blessed with riches that are worth more than material possessions that will pass away, for he receives the "crown of life." (*Note:* This crown is a victor's crown, a special reward for faithful endurance. It must not be confused with the eternal life which is the free gift of God to all who believe in the Lord Jesus Christ— *New Bible Commentary,* Eerdmans, 1953, p. 1120.)

11, 12. These last questions should help each person in your study group translate the principles of this passage into the substance of everyday experience.

Have enough pencils with you so that each person will be able to write a prayer. Be sure to make clear that the prayer time is a time when each will silently read her prayer to the Lord. If your group enjoys singing together, close with the song "Complete in Thee" printed at the end of the study.

2

How Can I Find Joy in Trial?

James 1:12–18

"Count it all joy, when you meet various trials." These are hard words with which James opens his book. We may say them with a smile through gritted teeth when the baby dumps his second bowl of cereal in fifteen minutes, or when the kitten claws a three-foot snag in our new drapes.

But the trials of Christians of the Dispersion were more harsh than these. Can we "count it all joy" when we lose our job, when a parent is diagnosed as having cancer, when a friend goes insane, when a child dies? Then the words take on a hollow edge of mockery. The trial becomes a true test of our faith.

James continues his discussion of the way a believer should meet trial. He defines the difference between "trial" and "temptation." He warns of the deviousness of sin. Then he closes with the utter trustworthiness of God.

By the end of today's study your view of joy may change. But so may your view of trial.

1. Each of us works for a variety of good goals which give our lives zest, meaning, and direction. These range from things like a home that we enjoy and educational experiences for our children that broaden their horizons (music lessons, Little League, a good college) to more time with people and better communication with those we love most. Try to get a meaningful response from each person since the answer to this question will be the basis for further discussion. But keep

your eye on the clock and push your group to stay within a five-minute time limit.

2. The phrase "tried and true" means that a person has been tested and proven to be steadfastly loyal or reliable, someone who is safe to trust under severe conditions. In this verse it is our love for God that is being tested by various pressures of life. These adverse circumstances are seen as a test which proves the genuineness of our commitment.

3. Evidently a trial is a circumstance that gives us the opportunity for choice. We can choose to obey God or to disobey Him when the chips are down, trust Him or take matters into our own hands, love Him whole-heartedly or vacillate in our loyalty. But temptation seems to be the gravitational pull of our own nature to question God or to do things our way instead of His. The source of temptation is to be sought not in God (or in circumstances), but in the individual himself. Temptation is the thought of sin entertained in our hearts, the desire to oppose God.

4. These words indicate subtlety, attractiveness, the use of appealing bait, something dangerous, or evil disguised as good. It may seem so good that we ignore or are blinded to the deadliness until it is too late. We all think of sin as being obvious and ugly; these words show it as appealing, attractive, seemingly worthwhile, but actually deadly.

5. The aspect of sin that is illustrated in these verses is that of the gradation from the slightly unorthodox to the frankly outrageous. It may be harmless flirting or incautious expressions of affection that slide gradually into outright immorality, or playing the angles with your income tax that turns into

calculated fraud. Each person is responsible before God to know his area of weakness and avoid the lure of temptation. Try to get your group to be illustrative and specific. One practical example will make more impression than many general fictitious possibilities.

6. Our strengths used apart from the guidance of God are always the most likely arena for defeat. Zeal for the Lord becomes self-righteous witch-hunting; concern for others can become mere meddlesomeness. The last question emphasized the progression from slightly different to flagrantly disobedient; this one shows the ability of good to become evil. The battleground is often our own drives, enjoyments, purposeful goals. This question coupled with the first one is meant to promote some constructive self-examination. Aim for this in your discussion.

7. Christians often subscribe to the viewpoint that material blessings and a trouble-free life are the necessary rewards of serving God. We are disheartened when we see worldly and unrighteous people leading a more enjoyable, comfortable, carefree life than many Christians. We begin to wonder if good things aren't actually a result of serving the world and doing things in a shrewd self-serving spirit. This passage says that all good things come from God's hand alone.

Many of us also tend to believe that if something is really enjoyable or would give us particular pleasure, there must automatically be something wrong with it. This passage indicates that God delights to give us things that are genuinely satisfying and lovely.

8. This is a personal experience question. Some suggestions could be grief, financial pressure, being too busy or

being bored, problem relationships with family or friends. Someone able to share a specific personal experience would be a help if it is not told in time-consuming detail.

9. Some of the responses indicated by these verses are that God is personally committed to our good. He has already taken the initiative to help us. There is a reliability and absolute certainty about Him, His promises, and His intentions.

10. A few suggestions might be: a sense of hopefulness and expectancy, a willingness to hang in there and to look for God's answers, some sense of purpose in these bad times, the lifting of our sense of aloneness, an ability to appreciate the things that are good about life and to thank God for them.

11. Suggestions should be specific and practical. Something I can say to God would be: 1) the positive things I believe about Him, and 2) an honest expression of the way I am feeling now. I might sing "Fairest Lord Jesus." In routine activities, a homemaker needs to keep the dishes washed and a commuter needs to catch the train each morning. An example of something to do to encourage joy would be to make a list of everything that has ever given pleasure (reading a book or going window shopping) and picking one to do each week. Take a friend to a new restaurant, for instance.

3

Is My Religion True?

James 1:18–27

Cults, false belief, watered-down faith, true religion. How can you tell the difference? How can I know if my own religion is real? This is the subject of James's first chapter.

One mark of true religion, James says, is that it allows the believer to endure trial. But, we may quickly counter, nearly every cult in history has experienced persecution—and its believers have endured, or died. So we must then look at the kind of endurance, the reasons behind enduring, and the results of endurance that make the real difference between Christian and cultist. It is to these distinctions that James points in the first half of chapter 1.

In the second section of this chapter, he trains his sights on a second criteria of true religion. True religion, says he, results in changed behavior. It is a faith of action. Once again we may raise our eyebrows at known cults and cite numerous changes in behavior, some bizarre, but changes none the less. And once again we must look carefully at the passage. Just what change does James suggest? What characterizes the behavior of a true believer?

As you prepare, pray for those who attend your group. Ask that God will prepare them to stand before the full-length mirror of His Word—and to walk away changed.

1. Enough answers to this question appear in the passage so that each member of your group ought to find something different. Possible responses include:

It is the word of truth (v. 18).
It is the agent by which God brings us to faith (v. 18).
It causes us to be first fruits (v. 18).
It is implanted in us (v. 21).
It is able to save our souls (v. 21).
It should result in action (v. 22).
It is a law (sets forth rules for living) (v. 25).
It gives liberty (v. 25).
It is perfect (v. 25).

2. Your group should answer all three questions though the order may be random.

3. If your group is slow to relate this question to the passage, you might point out the pivot words "for" of verse 20 and "therefore" of verse 21. Once a basis in the passage is firmly established, the group should feel free to discuss the practical implications of these questions.

4, 5. The words *receive, meekness, implanted,* are a basis for contrast.

Note: The word *meek* is often thought to mean "milk toast" or wishy-washy, but the biblical concept of meekness does not follow this pattern. Moses is referred to, in Numbers 12:3, as "very meek, more than all men that were on the face of the earth," yet he was a strong and fiery leader of over 600,000 men along with their families. *New Bible Commentary* defines meekness as "strength restrained" (p. 1126).

6, 7. If your group is slow to respond to this question, ask, "What qualities do a mirror and God's Word share?" Help the group look at the purposes of each.

8. This is a preliminary application question. As such it may be the most important thing that some of your group members take home with them. Allow ample time, at least ten minutes, to explore it.

9. Anyone who has begun to discipline a child in pretended anger and wound up genuinely angry, or who has argued a fuzzy case so fervently that he convinced himself, knows the self-deceit of too much talk. Your group may think of other examples. Encourage them to mention specific experiences. Shared laughter at this weakness held in common will lighten the tone of the discussion and will, at the same time, bring the teachings of this verse to your own front doors.

10, 11, 12. These verses reflect three evidences of true religion: control of the tongue, concern for the needy, and a life lived according to moral law. These define a life of discipline, service, and holiness.

13. Allow a few moments of silence for your group to collect their thoughts about a specific instance and a specific plan of action. Do not encourage sharing beyond the degree of trust that your group members have established with each other. (You can suggest that they not name the person or the situation, but only the step of change that they hope to initiate.) But do help them to be as personal as possible. Each response to this question should begin with the word "I," not "we" or "they."

You can bring the study to a close by reading the poem of confession by Luci Shaw, or by praying together for those who have shared the steps they hope to take in applying this passage.

4

How Do I Measure a Person's Worth?

James 2:1–13

One of the hardest jobs we Christians face is that of discovering the ways society's values have taken root in our lives so that we no longer reflect the values of our God. James says we do this when we respect people for the wrong reasons. We think financial success and power are important. We count wealth by material possessions rather than by spiritual resources. We show favor to people who have the wrong kind of riches.

God commands us to treat everyone alike—just the way we love ourselves (v. 8). We break this law and excuse our sin by saying, "That's just human nature. It's not a very important sin. After all, I didn't murder anyone or commit adultery."

The litmus test of our desire to obey God is our attitude toward other people. Do we really value people as God values them? God says not loving others is not loving others, no matter how it shows up.

This study is not about whether it is all right to count some people as special friends and enjoy their company most. But it does condemn the superficial, selfish ways we assign worth and show respect. We are to avoid the judgment system of the world. We are to treat all people with consideration and mercy. Each of us needs this kind of mercy from God. As His people, we must show it to others as well.

1. Use this question to discover and dramatize the facts of these verses. The Christians seem to have shown undeserved

honor to the rich and ignored the poor, even having them stand or sit on the floor. Encourage answers that specify what a visitor in this church would see, and quote what he might hear.

2. In answering this question, group members will need to examine and identify with the values and selfish needs that moved James's readers, because they influence us as well. Possible answers might be: They are children of a culture that respects money and admires success. They want to know people who have the power to help them. In a small, struggling church, there is respectability and protection in having influential people in the congregation. It is embarrassing to be associated with people who are scorned by society. (Consider what the "evil thoughts" in verse 4 might be.)

3. They claim to be God's people but do not live by God's evaluations. They show honor to their enemies instead of their friends.

4. A variety of answers are possible. Partiality promotes rivalry and ill feeling. If people most honored by the church are those with the least spiritual sensitivity, the church will be ineffectual.

5. Consider each of these persons separately. Read the list, then go back and mention them one by one, waiting for group members to give answers.

6. If Christ is the standard, everyone else is pale in comparison. We only have glory compared with one another; none of us has glory when compared with Christ. Any reason to boast comes from Him, not from our own worth.

7. Encourage personal, specific answers. How do we justify differences in the way we discipline our children, for instance? Some other preferences show in our attitude toward educational degrees, Christian celebrities, occupations, natural attractions, personal benefits.

Compare these answers to the information given in the passage, with particular reference to verses 5 and 6.

8. "You should love your neighbor as yourself." This command is found throughout Scripture. In the Old Testament it is implied in the last half of the Ten Commandments (Exodus 20:12–17), and stated explicitly in Leviticus 19:18. Jesus taught it (Mark 12:28–33) and so did Paul (Romans 13:8–10 and Galatians 5:14).

9. The law is broken just as completely when we fail to obey the command to love as it is when we fail to obey the command not to kill. One of the tests of our desire to obey God and submit to His lordship is our attitude toward our neighbor.

10. The law of freedom in Christ is a more sensitive test of our relation to God than the law of Moses. We are responsible not only for following a list of rules, but for spontaneously following Jesus Christ from the heart. We are responsible for knowing the Lord and responding to His desires and for knowing our brother and acting in his best interests. We are responsible for our attitudes as well as our actions. (This question may be omitted if you are short of time.)

11. Your group may have differing responses to this. However, James's argument seems to be that under God's righteous government, perfect obedience to His laws is required.

Justice is done when each person receives the reward or punishment he has earned with no partiality shown by God. However, on His great day of judgment, God will cause mercy to win over judgment, since all who are forgiven in Jesus Christ will be brought into His glory. We demonstrate the fact that we have experienced God's forgiveness and have recognized our own unworthiness by being ready to forgive others and show them mercy for His sake.

12. You may need to restate the royal law (v. 8) to be sure each person has it clearly in mind when you read this question. Some answers might be: I see I have enough food and am warm and comfortable. I find interesting things to do and try to look nice so others will respect me. I want to be proud of myself. I try to develop my talents and skills. I pay attention to me—my feelings and opinions.

A good place to use the optional reading, "How Do I Love Me?" is after your group has discussed the first part of this question.

Don't go into the second section of number 12 until each person has someone in mind. These names should not be shared, but the specific ways each one wishes to show love ought to be discussed.

5

Is My Faith Dead Or Alive?

James 2:14–26

Is salvation by faith alone, by works alone, or by both faith and works? Many people bring such questions to this passage. Because of its emphasis on works, it has split denominations. It may also cause division within your group. But carefully studied, it can clarify the Biblical conditions for salvation.

To avoid unnecessary argument, you may find it wise to clarify in your own mind just which issues this passage addresses and which it does not. The following observations may help.

1) The person who lives a good moral life apart from faith is not studied here. The question of whether such a person is saved simply is not addressed by the passage.

2) The person who *says* he has saving faith but whose life does not exhibit this faith is the prime target. What question, then, is James handling? "Is his kind of faith really saving faith?"

3) Therefore the passage deals with two kinds of faith: a faith without works and a faith that produces works. The question at issue becomes, "Which of these is saving faith?" We might also ask, "Does *saving* faith ever exist alone— apart from works?" With these points in mind you can help your group avoid fruitless tangents that cannot be answered in the passage; at the same time you can help them face the real issues addressed here.

Pray this week that your group members will have the patience necessary to reason through a passage heavily laced with doctrine. Pray that God will give them clear thinking on which to base the practical advice that follows in the Book of James. Pray particularly for any whom you fear may be harboring a shallow faith uncommitted to living in obedience to God's laws. Ask that God will reveal to them the danger of such self-delusion.

This study is a long study. It takes time to work through James's logic and understand it; there are more discussion questions than usual. Start promptly to give yourself time.

1. Encourage each person in your group to give some answer to this question. But keep it short—a popcorn session—not more than two or three minutes.

2. Answers include: This faith has no works attached, it sees need and offers no help, it offers good wishes without actions. It is dead. Be sure that your group notices the direct description "dead." That description will become important later in the study.

3. As your group looks again at the question of verse 14, "Can such faith save him?" (NIV), they might well ask, "Can a faith that produces no works possibly be the kind of faith that has repented of sin? Is that a life responding lovingly to God?"

4. If the group questions what knowledge is available to demons, ask them to read the words of a demon as he conversed with Christ in Luke 4:34.

5. Descriptive terms might include: shallow, barren, not genuine, incomplete, the same kind of faith that demons have.

Your group should begin to feel wary of any faith based

merely on acknowledgment of fact. The demons know all the facts of the Christian faith. They have chosen, however, not to act on this knowledge.

6. The lives of Abraham and Rahab.

7. It would not be said that Abraham had either faith alone or works alone. He proved his faith by his works, yet his works (sacrificing his son) were so demanding that no person could have done it without faith.

Additional notes on faith and works:

It is possible that someone in your group will bring up other passages in the New Testament that appear to contradict verse 24; Ephesians 2:8–10 and First John 2:3–6, for example. Properly understood, these passages will defend James's argument, not refute it.

In Ephesians 2, Paul is speaking about the work of Christ —his death in payment for our sin. So he concludes his argument (v. 8), "For by grace you have been saved through faith; and this is not your own doing, it is the gift of God—not because of works, lest any man should boast." But Paul hastens to add in verse 10, "For we are his workmanship, created in Christ Jesus for good works, which God prepared beforehand, that we should walk in them." Even in this passage where Paul speaks emphatically of God's gift of forgiveness through Jesus Christ, he points out that the faith receiving this gift will produce works. It is a gift of forgiveness that leads to works.

First John 2:3–6 is in the same vein, ending with, "By this we may be sure that we are in him: he who says he abides in him [Christ] ought to walk in the same way in which he walked."

The New Bible Dictionary, Eerdmans, 1962, reconciles Paul's and James's view of justification in this way:

> When James speaks of 'being justified,' he appears to be using the word in its more general sense of being vindicated, or proved genuine and right before God and men, in the face of possible doubt as to whether one was all that one professed. . . . James' point in this paragraph is simply that 'faith,' i.e. a bare orthodoxy, such as the devils have (v. 19), unaccompanied by good works, provides no sufficient ground for inferring that a man is saved. Paul would have agreed heartily (p. 686).

If your group seems to miss some of the important issues raised by question 7, try these alternate questions:

a. According to verses 22 and 23, on what basis was Abraham declared righteous?

b. How is verse 24 a summary of that statement?

8. If the answers center around emotions (like faith and love) you need to ask how these emotions can be identified by others. Force the group to be concrete and specific. You might want to ask, "What do you expect of a friend?"

9. The idea of Abraham being God's friend is an appealing one. It really gets to the emotional heart of the issue. A person who believes God has loved him, died for him, forgiven him, given him a new life, would delight to have God be able to call him "friend." You might be able to help your group answer this more practically if you prompt the discussion by asking, "In what way this week would you like to be a friend to God?"

10. Rahab's beliefs include:

—God had given the land to His people.

—She feared God's power.

—She knew that God had dried up the Red Sea to make a path for His people.

—She believed that God is Lord of the heavens above and also the earth.

Let your group pick out the actions of Rahab that were based on these beliefs.

11. Your group should find several qualities that these two characters held in common. They might also notice the difference in their stations. Abraham was chosen by God to be the father of the Jews. Rahab, a prostitute, was not even respectable among her own people, the pagan Canaanites.

12. Use this question to review the entire passage so that each person has clearly in mind the two kinds of faith and the qualities of each.

13. Second Corinthians 5:17 may be a help here.

14. Aim to have each member of your group answer this question in some way. We began the study by asking, "What use is your faith?" These questions give each person the satisfaction of beginning to notice how faith changes her life and of putting it more consciously into action.

The three examples of faith in action given by James are: giving physical help to the needy, Abraham's willingness to sacrifice his son, and Rahab's harboring spies. Areas of life that these might suggest for application could be: meeting the basic needs of someone else, letting God be Lord in our plans and in our family relationships, and letting God's law control our political and social decisions.

If personal response is slow, refer the group to these examples in the passage for ideas.

Pray together, asking God's help for each person who has shared a specific plan to put faith into action.

6

Do I Have Tongue Trouble?

James 3:1–12

"Sticks and stones may break my bones, but words can never hurt me," goes the old nursery rhyme.

Is that so?

Consider these comments: "Have you heard about Sue? I'm so worried about her. Her marriage is a real disaster."

"I'm sorry, Eric. I know I said we were going to the zoo today, but Mommy has too many important things to do to get away."

"Mike, have you ever realized what a talent you have for explaining things? You make something complicated sound easy. That's a real gift."

Just words, but . . .

*   *   *

Words can be life changing. They can encourage and support or they can destroy. Broken bones heal, but wounds caused by words may last a lifetime.

Not only do words affect other people, but they affect the

speaker. Blowing off steam may actually make a person angrier instead of relieving tension. Telling a white lie to get out of a social engagement may chàin the teller to the house all day to keep from being caught.

In this passage of Scripture, James talks to those whose whole ministry is words, those who want to teach. He warns them about the special responsibility placed on teachers. Then he goes on to show what potent, long-lasting effects words can have.

1. This question is to help the group begin to realize that unguarded speech reveals our real self. Let several people answer, but keep an eye on the time, with the rest of the study in mind. Don't get carried away with supper table anecdotes. Aim for descriptive *words* with a brief illustration, rather than descriptive *stories*.

2. A teacher is responsible for the depth, breadth, and accuracy of his knowledge. It should go well beyond that necessary for merely presenting the lesson. He is responsible for continuing to be a learner and for being able to practice what he teaches. He must be skilled in performance as well as in theory. He should be a good communicator and inspirer. He is responsible for the truth and his ability to present it without distortion. He must know and understand his pupils, what they need and are ready to learn. He is responsible to God for saying everything that God has shown him, without change or addition.

3. Your group should consider both the attractiveness of the job and the possible consequences of poor teaching. Because it is prestigious, many people are likely to wish to teach. Sometimes people want to teach because they are

proud of their own knowledge and wish to display it. But it is also a job that can attract misfits. The results of bad teaching have far-reaching consequences. A teacher influences many people. When the subject being taught has eternal consequences, this influence is particularly serious.

4. Direct discussion toward verse 2. Speech seems almost to have a will of its own. Quite without wanting to, we display our prejudices, bad temper, and poor judgment. What is inside seems to come out in our speech at one time or another. So if a person can speak only when appropriate and what he does say consistently reveals spiritual wisdom, he shows both the maturity of self-control and the maturity of changed character. The word *body* may be an indirect reference to the Body of Christ. A person who speaks both truthfully and graciously is one who is competent for church leadership.

5. The examples are the bit in the horse's mouth, the rudder that controls a large ship, and a flame that has the power to start a full blaze. In all of these the major characteristic is the great influence in proportion to the very small size. The horse is guided and directed with very little force or effort, as is the ship. The tongue itself can be directed and its direction depends on the purpose of the pilot. It can guide and control forces much stronger than itself. The rudder, for instance, takes a powerful wind or sea that could wreck the ship. It uses these forces effectively and creatively.

The tongue, like a small flame, can kindle growth or destruction, inspire courage or dejection. It can bring light and warmth to our relationships. Something relatively insignificant becomes a powerful force.

6, 7. A number of people in the group will probably remember one conversation that has affected their lives. This could be as simple as a friend who, with a thoughtful remark lifted a black mood, or a teacher who pointed out abilities that led to a career, or a Christian who said a word or two that started a search for God and led to conversion. Most of us have had experience with speaking gently or kindly and finding that our anger was gentled in the process, or in telling someone the truth and finding that it opened up a whole new relationship. (Negative effects might also be mentioned, as when irresponsible promises or lying have affected our actions, or when anger, pretended in order to impress, has become the real thing. However, since the impact of these verses is mostly positive, concentrate on moving the discussion toward positive personal examples as well.)

8. A destructive fire is the first example, something out of control and on the rampage. A stain, or dye, that spreads and colors everything it touches would be the second. It is like a drop of red food coloring in a glass of water. The idea of the cycle of nature might indicate a life-long problem, not something that is temporary or merely a stage of development as we grow up. It is a devilish force. Like the ship, it is accomplishing the will of another, but unlike the ship it is a wildly unguided force once it is in motion. The third example is the wild beast. These are by nature wild and uncontrolled, but with effort man can bring them under control. The tongue is wilder than that; it is not capable of being tamed. The picture is of a powerful, destructive, evil force that can bring death.

9. Give people a minute to think and then ask for responses. These should be from personal experience and as brief and specific as possible. The illustrations are merely suggestions to help the group think of actual situations.

10. Water is either pure or it is brackish. There is no "mostly pure" water. If our praise to God is tainted by our uncharitable speech to others, it is no longer pure praise.

11. It might help for each person to write an answer to this question before sharing.

12. This is a practical review of all the areas you have touched on in your discussion. Members of the group will likely have been most affected by different parts of the study. Responses should be varied and personal. Some members may wish to be more thoughtful of a particular person. Others may be aware of unloving attitudes, while still others may be more concerned about showing disrespect by gossip, impatience, sarcasm, or unkind jokes. Everyone will likely want her speech to show more appreciation.

7

How Can I Live Out God's Wisdom?

James 3:13–18

Just as Lesson 5 speaks of two kinds of faith, so today's passage speaks of two kinds of wisdom. The sources are opposite and so are the results. Only one type comes from God and grows into action that pleases Him.

Today's study should help your group discover what wisdom is, so the members may better discern who is truly wise, and so they may evaluate whether their own actions demonstrate godly wisdom. Pray that the people in your group will be willing to take an honest look at themselves as they study God's criteria for these answers.

1. If your group is small, let everyone respond to this question. Larger groups will benefit from a few sample answers as four or five people respond.

2, 3. Earthly wisdom is marked by bitter jealousy, selfish ambition, disorder, and vile practice. Its origin is unspiritual, devilish.

Godly wisdom is pure, peaceable, gentle, open to reason, full of mercy and good fruits, without uncertainty, sincere. Its origin is from above.

Some groups will feel hesitant about reading characteristics that are so obvious. To say them aloud, however, helps everyone take notice of the particular items. Otherwise, the terms are likely to blur into a hodgepodge, leaving only a vague impression of good as opposed to bad.

4, 5. Spend at least ten minutes here so that the group has adequate time to see that the seemingly harmless characteristics of ambition and jealousy can bring about serious consequences. Group members need to be specific enough in their examples to show that these are everyday sins Christians are likely to commit. They also need to see where these sins can lead.

6. The goal here is to recognize our own spiritual ambitions. (We all ought to have some if we are growing in our faith.) But as we admit to ourselves and others where we are

headed, we also need to examine the possible pitfalls so that we can develop spiritually without creating disorder around us. Again encourage your group to be as specific as possible. For example, "I would like to keep a notebook of prayers reflecting what God has taught me about Himself," is more to the point than "I want to live a better life."

If the group has difficulty talking about this spontaneously, ask each person to write down three spiritual ambitions, then share one with the group. Don't forget to talk about possible pitfalls.

7, 8. The contrast in ways a person relates to other people should be fairly obvious from the description in the passage. Be sure that your group goes beyond simply restating the facts. The group should talk about how these practices would affect interpersonal relationships.

As for results, earthly wisdom ends in disorder; godly wisdom in righteousness and peace.

The way a person relates to God is less obvious. Your group might suggest that a person possessing earthly wisdom might deceive himself, thinking that any wisdom must be from God. This would make true knowledge of God impossible. Or the group might notice that a person with wisdom from God is "open to reason." Therefore he is quick to learn more from God, either through His Word or through His people.

9. Have group members point out specific words in the text as they answer this question.

10. Leave at least ten or fifteen minutes for your group to interact with this question. If your group is comfortable praying together, close by praying about the situations they have just shared.

8

How Do I Get What I Want?

James 4:1–10

"You only go around once in life, so grab all the gusto . . ." Happy figures dance across the screen, smiling, nodding—and grabbing.

James paints a different picture of that philosophy. He talks about coveting, murder, fighting, wars. Suddenly the dancing figures look like cardboard cutouts draped in tarnished tinsel.

But James also presents an alternative: We may submit ourselves (and our possessions and our needs) to God. We may draw near to Him and know Him. Then as we are humble before God, He takes charge of our reputation. We will be exalted, not by grabbing at passing objects and opportunities—but by reaching for God Himself.

As you study this week, reevaluate the people, objects, and activities that are most important to you. Consider submitting each one of these to God.

Lesson 8 is somewhat shorter than the others. This is to allow fifteen minutes of guided silent prayer at the close of the discussion. See instructions at the end of this study.

1. Answers may range from methods of violence and trickery through subtle emotional tricks. You might encourage group members to remember methods they themselves use to get their way, but don't confine the discussion to this.

2. Be sure the group uses the whole passage. (You should be able to find eight or ten causes for fighting.) These will help

get the feel for the whole passage, laying groundwork for the rest of the discussion.

3. Answers to this question should show not only the intense conflict between individuals but also the internal conflict within the individual.

4. These verses show selfish, self-centered people. If they consider God at all, he is only a means to their own ends. Even in church they do things their own way, for their own reasons, using whatever methods they choose.

"Unfaithful creatures" carries the connotation of prostitution. God demands total loyalty from His followers. To form the kind of alliance with the world described here is like being unfaithful to one's husband.

5. An example of the kind of answer you are looking for might be desiring to teach a "successful" Sunday school class when the real motive is to enhance one's reputation as a spiritual leader. Members of your group may be aware of some of their own wrong motives. (What are some of yours?)

6. For the first part of the question, be sure answers come from the text. Answers to the second part are a mixture of textual answers (we lose God's grace and favor, and gain His opposition) and experiential answers (we gain the freedom of doing things our way, but lose the satisfaction of God's companionship).

7. Be sure your discussion group covers attitude, methods, and outcome.

8. A person might well try to get what he wants by com-

bining worldly methods with God's methods. He would hope to reap the benefits of both and stay on good terms with each. Problems are obvious. It leads to instability, as James 1:8 recalls. We risk becoming an enemy of God. Such procedure is like being the third man in a business partnership where the other two partners have opposite goals, attitudes, and methods from each other.

If your group members can discuss specific situations in which they are tempted to juggle worldly methods with God's methods of meeting needs, the danger of double-mindedness will become more real.

9, 10. These two questions deal with the aspects of being on God's side but renouncing Satan's way. Instead of resisting God we are to come close to Him. As we come close to Him, we will find we need to change our actions, commit our affections, become single-minded in our service, and take on God's view of sin. In running from Satan, we desert the "territory" God has given us to take charge of; we view our resources in Christ as insufficient to meet Satan's strength. When we stand up to Satan we affirm our allegiance to God and our trust in His Lordship. Then we have the satisfaction of engaging in successful battle. The attitude and the results are different.

11. In this answer you are looking both for what God will do and for what the individual will do.

12. Silent prayer. (Allow fifteen minutes for this section—at least two minutes for each meditation and prayer period.)

The time will go more smoothly if your procedure is clear before you begin to pray. This is to be a directed time of silent prayer. You as the leader will mention four separate areas, or topics, for prayer, allowing time after each for meditation and silent prayer. Then the group will pray aloud in unison the prayer in the study guide (page 55). The following comments to the group will help your time be worshipful and effective.

James says that as we draw near to God He will draw near to us. Let's spend time now drawing near to God in silent prayer. We'll use the areas suggested by the passage. I'll read aloud an area and allow time for meditation and silent prayer before going on to the next. There will be four areas in all. Then we'll pray aloud together the prayer written at the end of the discussion questions.

If you cannot honestly pray as suggested, tell the Lord so. You might ask Him to change your heart.

1) Acknowledge to God that everything you have comes from Him, and offer it back to Him. First, your skills. Name them and offer them in His service. (Pause for the group to do this.)

Next, the people you love most. Name them and give them to Him. (Pause for prayer.)

Now think of your most prized possession and offer it to Him. (Pause.)

2) Repent. Tell God of the ways you have tried to mix His way and the world's way to get what you want. (Pause.)

3) Ask God for what you now think you need. Ask Him to reveal whether your view is different from His. (Pause.)

4) Praise God. Thank Him that He has control over your need and your reputation. Thank Him that He will exalt you. (Pause.)

Unison prayer:

> Lord of all power and might, who art the author
> and giver of all good things; Graft in our hearts the
> love of thy Name, increase in us true religion,
> nourish us with all goodness, and of thy great
> mercy keep us in the same; through Jesus Christ our
> Lord. Amen.

—*The Book of Common Prayer*, 1781

9

Are My Plans God's Plans?

James 4:11–17

Today, tomorrow, next year . . . Plans for the future. We all
make them. Sometimes we order our lives around them. But
occasionally our carefully structured plans come crashing
down like a house of cards around our ears. What happens
then? Do we, like Job's wife, want to curse God and die? Or
do we look to God as the Lord of even our fallen plans, the
One who brings stability as we sit surrounded by the remains
of our paper house?

Today's study begins with arrogance: arrogance toward
one another, arrogance toward God's laws, arrogance about
our own life and our plans for it. And it ends with submission
to a Lord: Jesus Christ, Lord of a life that in the long view is

nothing more than a mist and Lord of our carefully laid plans for that life.

And once we see ourselves as servants to a Lord, the Lord of the universe, it's hard to be arrogant about a house of cards.

1. See how many people you can get to respond to this question. Each person who hears her voice early in the study will feel more a part of the discussion. Answers include: Arrogance speaks evil against others (v. 11), judges other Christians (v. 11), judges the law (v. 11), plans over-confidently for tomorrow (vv. 13–14), views life too highly (v. 14), knows to do good but fails to do it (v. 17).

2. The person described in verses 11 and 12 believes three things about himself: He is better than his brother; his own judgment is better than the law; he is a contemporary of God.

3. Review the two passages suggested and compare them with James 4:11. James once again treats the now familiar theme of sins of the tongue.

The "law" of verse 11 probably refers to the royal law of James 2:8. If we speak evil against someone, we obviously do not love that person as much as we love ourselves.

4. Get several responses. Try to work toward specific answers, particularly those that reflect a devious, undercover way of speaking evil. These might include sharp criticism, belittling someone, or other verbal attacks on a person's self-worth.

5. The mistakes fall generally into two categories: Arrogance toward life and arrogance toward God. As the group members point out findings from the passage, help them to

see these major categories. A few follow-up questions might help them reflect on their findings. You could ask, "What were the people doing? What was wrong with it? What false assumptions have they made about God?"

6. Many people accept casually the idea that if they receive Jesus merely as their Savior from sin they are assured a home in heaven. This may be a delusion. Jesus is both Lord and Savior. It is not possible to have a piece of Him without having all of Him. If Jesus is not their Lord, then neither is He their Savior. Sin at root is rejecting God as the rightful Ruler of our lives and placing ourselves on the throne. To repent of sin is to receive not only Jesus' payment for our sin, but to turn our lives over to Him as the rightful king.

As your group discusses what it means to have a lord, these ideas ought to emerge: Accepting Jesus as Lord admits that He is my Ruler. He has the right to command me. I no longer make decisions without reference to what my Lord wants of me because He has a prior claim. He can take me away from my own pursuits and send me on His. He has my allegiance; I would never side with my Lord's enemies. Because Jesus is a wise and loving Lord, I trust Him. If I am in difficulty, I can appeal to Him for help. He will grant protection and fair judgment.

7. The most obvious meaning is in terms of life's transience. However, there are other meaningful similarities. Your group may mention that life is unpredictable, transparent, inconsequential, uncontrolled, appears and disappears. This passage does not teach that life is worthless, but helps put it in the perspective of eternity.

In answer to the second question, look again at the way these people planned their lives.

8. Look back at the words you used to describe life in the previous question. Then discuss specific ways Jesus brings a steadiness in spite of that particular quality of life.

For example: Life is short—even seventy years is short in the span of universal time—however, for the Christian, life is eternal, beginning at the moment he accepts Christ as Savior and Lord and extending into an eternity in heaven.

9. Plan enough time so that several people can respond to these two questions. Though these questions form the basis for application, they will not of themselves bring about a discussion of specific application; so save fifteen minutes or more for the last two questions.

10. Allow a couple of minutes for writing, then let each person share one plan for tomorrow and one for the distant future.

11. If this passage of James has done its work, you should see some difference between the way people have reacted in the past when their plans did not work out and in their attitudes toward future plans. If Jesus is our Lord, He is Lord over smashed hopes and broken plans. Our plans can be more flexible, since we know that He has a master plan for our lives. Because He is a loving Lord, His plans for us are good.

Note: People who study this passage are likely to fall into two categories: They are over-planners or they are under-planners. They will each bring their own methods of planning (or not planning) and view the passage in relation to these methods.

The over-planner may say, "Life is precious; we ought to plan ever more carefully. Our Lord holds us responsible for the way we use our limited time."

The under-planner says, "Life is inconsequential and so are our plans. We must be flexible. Don't plan at all, or only the minimum; don't come unglued if your plans don't work out."

Much can be gained by each of these sides hearing the other. The over-planner needs to learn flexibility and the under-planner needs to learn responsibility. So while the discussion may become heated, if each side listens to the other, everyone should benefit.

10

Do My Possessions Cry Out Against Me?

James 5:1–12

Sometimes it seems as though God really must be dead, or at least sleeping. If He's in His heaven, why *isn't* all right with the world? Why is it that the rich get richer while the poor get poorer? Why doesn't God do something about exploitation, oppression, and indifference?

In this chapter, James declares that God is not an uninterested spectator. He sees the fraud, deceit, and corruption. He is not blind to the wasteful luxury that adds up to social cruelty. His judgment is certain; so certain that the indifferent rich ought to weep and howl in dread of it.

On the other hand, those who are waiting for the Lord can take courage, knowing that all wrongs will be righted. This is the conviction that will give hope and endurance. Why should we be irritable, anxious, and critical of one another when we know the Judge is standing at the door? He will judge our hard-heartedness as well as theirs.

Pray that, as you study together this week, members of your group who need encouragement will be strengthened for patient well-doing. Pray also that all of you will see ways in which you are indifferent to injustice and oppression, and that you will find practical ways to help.

1. Have the group members go straight through these six verses and mention all the reasons for distress that they can find.

2. The rotted riches, moth-eaten garments, and tarnished money show a lavish luxury. The people had more than they could use. Their wealth had been gained in corrupt ways. They held back just wages and used social oppression. They pampered themselves and failed to extend mercy to the oppressed. Their treasure was corrupted by the methods used to get it and by the use that was made of it.

3. Possessions were important for their own sake; people collected and hoarded things, gloating over owning them. Things were a form of security, protection against hard times, to be trusted more than God. Possessions were more important than people; people were "used" but possessions were cherished. Pleasure was a higher value than mercy or righteousness. Possessions had become the lord of their lives.

4, 5. The phrase "last days" implies the end of an existing way of life. Whether the judgment is by a conquering nation that will plunder their goods or by the return of the Lord who will use their treasure to condemn them, wealth is not going to do them any good. They have built the wrong bulwark against disaster.

6. The farmer waiting for harvest: Judgment will occur when the Lord comes. Waiting will establish their righteousness and their oppressors' sin. The crop will be ripe.

The prophets: The prophets spoke God's Word to an unbelieving world in a situation that made their words seem incredible. By remaining true to God's truth they saw His Word accomplished and were vindicated as "true prophets." Delay of the Lord's return will establish Christians' faithfulness. We can wait, knowing that despite present evidence to the contrary, we will be proven true.

Job: Because of his perseverance, Job was given a unique encounter with God and material blessing as well.

These three examples show that Christians will see justice, vindication, and blessing if they have the patience to wait for the Lord's return.

7. Be sure the group members don't go on before they find all the answers. These form a base for the rest of the study.

8. Knowing that the believers all belong to the Lord might help them support each other in trial. These instructions might also provide the following: Encouragement to grow in faith and maturity, since there is certain hope; a sense of humility and a readiness to try to understand others and work out difficulties; a trustful, humble, dependent attitude toward God; a desire not to take Him for granted, but to please Him. The knowledge that Jesus is coming as judge might make a person much more careful not to be guilty of sin in his relations with other Christians.

9. God's delay of judgment gives sinners every chance to repent. That God does right the wrongs shows He is compassionate toward those who are being wronged. He doesn't ignore injustice.

10. This question needs responses that are personal. Your group could profitably consider how we might become more ready for Jesus' appearing—in our relation to Him, in righting wrongs around us, in relationships with other Christians.

11. It will help you in leading the discussion of this question if you take the time to become acquainted with current issues in your community. Look through recent issues of the community paper, talk to someone in the League of Women Voters, find out what issues are being discussed by the school board or city council. What needs are there at school? Or on your own block?

Have your group list a number of situations at the local level. (County, state, national issues may be too abstract for personal involvement.) You may experience some resistance to discussing practical measures, since all of us try to avoid involvement when we weigh the cost of specific action. But you are not necessarily aiming at instant commitment; practical, creative alternatives for consideration will be a good start. If, however, your group is able to form a cohesive plan of action, you might adopt as a project the righting of one specific injustice in your community.

11

Why Do I Need Other Christians?

James 5:13–20

"Who needs a church? I can worship God just as well alone on a mountain top—or in my own back yard, for that matter. I don't need stained glass and organ music and padded pews and pious faces. In fact, I don't need other Christians at all. I'll stay out of church and spare myself the hassle."

Heard it? Admired it? Said it?

James 5 doesn't say much about stained glass and padded pews, and some of the other accouterments of today's churches; but it says a lot about believers needing each other. When and why and how. You might discover that going it alone in your Christian faith isn't going much of anywhere at all. You might even discover that the support system designed by God for His people is one of loving concern, a system you can alternately draw on and contribute to. James's view of the church is of something far more valuable than pews and glass.

1. Don't get into a detailed discussion of this question, as you will treat it more thoroughly later in the study. One-phrase answers, based on various sections of the passage, are sufficient here.

2. Be sure that your group accounts for all three characters: the sick man, the elders, the Lord. Their answers should show that they noticed who calls, who comes, what they do, who heals, and why.

3. As you look at the responsibilities given here to the elder, these and other qualities might come to mind: He should be spiritually mature; he should be familiar with prayer; he should know how to pray with faith; he should be able to hear sins; he should be willing to drop everything on short notice and come.

If your group needs to have the office of elder more clearly defined, see First Timothy 3:1–7 and Titus 1:5–9.

4. Answers to this question call for fitting into our framework the procedure described in these verses of what Scripture teaches about the nature of God and His expectations for His people. Your group should think of several answers. They might include: The sick man's humility in calling for help; the mutual dependence of believers; the expression of faith on the part of the sick man and the elders; an attitude of trust in God even during illness; the recognition of a possible connection between sin and sickness; an understanding that God desires righteousness in His people—so He expects confession as a route to forgiveness; and He grants power in prayer to the righteous believer.

5. Answers should form an outline of the passage.

a) Christians are to praise God together in times of joy (v. 13).

b) They are to pray for healing for each other in times of sickness (vv. 14–15).

c) They are to confess their sins to one another and, together, to God (v. 16).

d) They are to increase each other's faith by looking at God's past answers to prayer (vv. 17–18).

e) They are to shepherd each other when there is temptation to wander from the truth (vv. 19–20).

6. Your group should think of several values of confession. Confession is most appropriate when we have wronged another believer. It will restore our relationship. In broader settings, confession might help us stay away from a particular sin, since we have stated aloud exactly what that sin is. Confession brings the prayer support of another believer; confession might also bring that believer's counsel in helping us overcome that sin (he may have battled that same sin in the past). Confession can help us believe that we are forgiven (the other believer can remind us that we have brought it to God together and He has forgiven us).

Confession to each other also has obvious dangers. If your group shows signs of falling into these, remind them that our confession must never endanger the reputation or well-being of any other person.

7. A righteous person knows God; he knows what God expects in prayer. He is accustomed to praying and is more likely to ask for that which is within God's will. He is aware of the many scriptural conditions for strength in prayer and he obeys these. Perhaps because he walks daily with God, God is more likely to honor his prayer.

8. See verses 17 and 18.

9. Try to get five or six people to respond here. Help them to interact with each other's ideas.

10. Each person in your group should respond to at least one section of this question.

11. If yours is a group within a church, you might table this question now and spend a whole class period on it next week.

Then your class can present its evaluation and suggestions to your church board.

If your group represents a mixture of churches, you can treat the question more briefly, with an objective of each person helping his own church to better provide the support described in this passage. If that seems totally impossible for some group members, they may wish to consider whether they are in the right church. If not, consider what criteria they might use to select a more biblically structured congregation.

12

How Can I Know If I'm a Christian?

Ephesians 2:1–10

James has written his letter to Jewish Christians throughout the world. It is a letter of pastoral encouragement and rebuke. He has assumed that the essential doctrines of the Christian faith are known to his readers, and he is concerned that all their actions should witness to their new life in Christ and glow with Christian love.

Life in Christ, however, is not merely a matter of conforming to God's law. It is instead a whole new source of life. The Old Testament prophets said the difference was like receiving hearts of flesh for hearts of stone. Jesus told Nicodemus it was like being born again—alive to a whole new world. The apostle Paul says that though we are used to thinking that all people are alive until they die, the fact is that all people are dead unless they are made alive. This week you will study how dead people come alive.

Maybe some of the members of your study group are not alive yet. Perhaps they are trying to obey God, to put the instructions of James into practice, with dead spirits. Pray that as you study this passage in Ephesians together that God will show them their deadness and cause them to turn to Him for life.

1. This question is both a review of James and a transition to Ephesians. Have each member of your group mention one thing that has been particularly meaningful from the study of James. However, James's standards are so high that it would be impossible to feel adequate to the job. A non-Christian would find this particularly difficult. The study in Ephesians helps us understand why this is true.

2. People are all dead until they have been made alive. Usually we think of a person being alive until he dies, but here it is just the opposite. A person is dead until made alive. All of us were once dead. This was a death caused by walking in sins and trespasses—a lifestyle characterized by disregard for God. The particular characteristics are found in the specifics of the first three verses. After the phrases in the passage have been discovered and mentioned, have the group members summarize them in their own words.

3. Have your group suggest common modern attitudes and actions. "Following the course of this world" (v. 2) could be typified by pride and love of material things. A spirit of disobedience is usually exhibited by self-centered decisions, a disregard for restrictions, an insistence on my own rights

without regard for others. Desires of the flesh are usually thought to be sexual, but are just as easily a love of food, comfort, or entertainment. Desires of the mind might be daydreams, preoccupation with intellectual attainments, or an aggressive drive for self-fulfillment and prestige.

4. In these verses, "dead" seems to indicate someone whose life is governed not by love of God but by love for himself and the world. He has chosen to ignore God's values and has followed other loyalties. He is spiritually dead.

5. We need a God who is merciful, because we have been disobedient and deserve His anger. God must be loving, because we are very unlovely if the picture of the first three verses is correct. We need His generosity and kindness, because we have nothing to bring to Him to recommend us—we are impoverished. And we need a God who is creative, since we are dead and need to be created anew.

6. The passage says that in love and mercy He took us when we were dead and made us alive. We now share Christ's aliveness. He raised us up and has given us a heavenly home with Christ. Instead of a life that is focused on superficial and fleshly concerns, He will show us the riches of His kindness. Life will not end but will continue for ages. All this is action which God has initiated and accomplished through Jesus Christ.

7. According to this passage, He has saved us from the deadness of life lived without knowing Him, caused by our sins and trespasses. He has saved us to real aliveness—being loved and in love with Him. He has given us the gift of life in Jesus Christ and saved us from living death.

8. In the first three verses, you, the reader, are the acting person. As the reader, I am walking in sins, following the world and the prince of power. I am living in my own feelings and desires. In the verses from 4 on, God becomes the acting person. The implication is that I can get myself into the mess, but only God can get me out.

9. Those works in verse 9 are the ones that a person does, hoping to win favor with God and to save himself. The works in verse 10 are those which God has appointed for us to do as His new, alive creation. They arise out of our aliveness to God and our love and loyalty to Him. They come from a grateful heart rather than a fearful or proud one. They do not save, but are the result of having been saved.

10. The loyalties of the dead as described in the first few verses are to the world, to a spirit that is disobedient to God, and to his own creature comforts and rights. You would expect an alive person to respond in loving gratitude to his Savior and Creator. An alive person would be eager to be like Him in kindness to unlovely ones and in loyalty to others who are now alive with Him. He would be likely to have a world-view of life rather than just a self-view of life. You'd expect him to be on God's side in a spiritual battle.

11. This false confidence blinds my eyes to the gravity of the problem and my own helplessness, and thereby prevents me from receiving the gift God offers me. The repetition of the phrase "in Christ" in the Ephesian passage emphasizes the point that life comes only as a gift to us as we trust God's work for us in Jesus Christ.

12. Examples of aliveness might include: The delight of

His presence, a new sense of direction, good things to do that are particularly mine, sensitivity to what is good and right, pleasure in doing right, a new enjoyment of the created world since I am not enslaved by it. Your group will think of others.

This is the kind of question that can help non-Christians see that, in fact, they may not have a real newness of life. If you have non-Christians in your group, you might ask some of the Christians to think about this question in advance so that they will speak of some of the things that are most meaningful to them.

13. This passage emphasizes that life is something that God gives to us. Answers to the question should fall into four categories: 1) In order to receive this gift a person would need to recognize he was dead and unable to save himself. 2) The passage keeps repeating that this salvation is intimately connected to Jesus Christ; verse 8 says it is through faith in what God has done for us that we are able to receive His gift of salvation. 3) Our loyalties will be so drastically changed that we need to count the cost and acknowledge our indebtedness to Christ by turning all areas of our life over to Him. A person cannot be half alive. 4) Since this life involves a relationship with a living person, Jesus Christ, we need to tell Him that we want His gift and are ready to receive it from Him. And thank Him for it.

Create an atmosphere by the close of this study that encourages anyone who is ready to make a personal commitment to Jesus Christ to make this decision, or at least to continue to think about it. Then follow up. A Christian in the group might invite this person to have coffee, so that they can discuss, one to one, their reactions to the Book of James and to this study in particular.

OTHER BOOKS BY THESE AUTHORS

By Carolyn Nystrom and Margaret Fromer
  Acts: Missions Accomplished

By Margaret Fromer and Sharrel Keys
  Letters to Timothy
  Letters to the Thessalonians
  Let's Pray Together
  Genesis: Walking with God
  Genesis: Called by God

By Carolyn Nystrom
  Forgive Me If I'm Frayed Around the Edges
  Mark: God on the Move
  Acts: The Church on the Move
  Romans: Christianity on Trial
  I Learn About the Bible
  Angels and Me
  I Learn to Pray
  Who Is God?
  Who Is Jesus?
  The Spirit in Me.